Fake News

A POCKET PRIMER

T0395046

WRITTEN BY
CHRIS STOKEL-WALKER

EDITED BY
FLORENCE WARD

Fake News: A pocket primer
First edition

Published in 2025 by
Hoxton Mini Press, London
Copyright © Hoxton Mini Press
2025. All rights reserved.

Text by Chris Stokel-Walker
Edited by Florence Ward
Production design and additional
artwork by Dom Grant
Series design by Tom Etherington
Cover illustration by Lan Truong
Proofreading by Zoë Jellicoe

Thank you to all of the individuals
and institutions who have provided
images and arranged permissions.
While every effort has been made to
trace the present copyright holders
we apologise in advance for any
unintentional omission or error,
and would be pleased to insert the
appropriate acknowledgement in
any subsequent edition.

A CIP catalogue record for this
book is available from the
British Library.

ISBN: 978-1-914314-85-8

Printed and bound by Ozgraf, Poland

Manufacturer: Hoxton Mini Press,
104 Northside Studios, 16-29
Andrews Road, London, E8 4QF
www.hoxtonminipress.com

Represented by: Authorised Rep
Compliance Ltd., Ground Floor,
71 Lower Baggot Street, Dublin,
D02 P593, Ireland
www.arccompliance.com

Hoxton Mini Press is an envi-
ronmentally conscious publisher,
committed to offsetting our carbon
footprint. This book is 100 per cent
carbon compensated, with offset
purchased from Stand For Trees.

Every time you order from our
website, we plant a tree:
www.hoxtonminipress.com

Introduction:
Why should we care
about fake news?

Between Donald Trump hurling disinformation at globally broadcast events and your friends and relatives contributing to the morass of misinformation on social media, it can be difficult not to feel disheartened about fake news. You might even think you aren't susceptible to it. When the world feels rife with misguided statements, exaggerations and outright lies, it's tempting to turn a blind eye and log off.

But burying our collective heads in the sand won't work. Fake news has become impossible to ignore. It spreads like weeds, choking the life out of society as we know it. Both disinformation (the deliberate concoction of falsehoods) and misinformation (the innocent, unwitting sharing of falsity) are potent, but in different ways. Combined, they create a world where truth is constantly contested.

And things are getting worse. AI makes it increasingly tough to separate fact from fiction. AI-generated images, audio and video are already blurring the line between reality and unreality. Trust – in media, government institutions and, yes, each other – is collapsing.

Yet, for all the issues social media and tech like AI are causing – supercharging the production and dissemination of fake news – the concept is hardly a modern issue. Its roots go back thousands of years. In fact, from the moment humans started communicating, they also started lying. Ancient civilisations grappled with scuttlebutt, rumours and innuendo, just as we do today. We're instinctively drawn to sensational stories, to believe what aligns with our worldview and to share information that evokes a strong response – it's just how our brains are hardwired. From the Pope in a puffer jacket (p.116) to scurrilous hearsay on the school run, this compulsion exists in all of us – even if we think we're smarter than most.

All of this matters because knowing what truth is, and being able to appeal to it, is central to democracy. The internet and social media democratised access to information. But that openness also made it easier to spread falsehoods, undermine trust in institutions, erode civil discourse and destabilise the democratic process. In our era of information overload, it's incumbent on us all – as informed citizens – to discern fact from fiction.

That's why this book exists. It's intended to guide you through the challenging environment of fake news and misinformation, acting as a handy guide to distinguishing what's real and what isn't through the lens of some of the most troubling examples of disinformation from the past and the present – with a look towards the future, too.

What is
fake news?

The *Weekly World News* was a tabloid newspaper publishing
entirely fictional, satirical news. The paper was renowned
for its outlandish, attention-grabbing headlines. If only
all fake news was as harmless and entertaining.

What exactly is fake news?

It's a phrase bandied about by everyone these days, often ironically. At its heart, fake news is the way in which false or misleading information is presented as real. But the term has been co-opted for partisan political aims and means many things to many people, depending on your political persuasion and trust in the traditional media ecosystem.

Fake news has polluted the well of public discourse for all time. People want to deceive the public, to push an agenda or make money from sensational storytelling. There are different degrees of fake news, too: from the amplification of an element of truth to make it more outlandish, to outright lies.

But it's an issue that has become more prevalent as social media and other tech advances have made it easier to prepare, present and promote false information to the unwitting public. And as we'll learn throughout the coming pages, it can happen almost anywhere, about anything – and can be produced by anybody.

Why do we believe it?

Fake news pushes our emotional buttons. Even the most critical thinker or deepest sceptic can be hoodwinked by its ability to needle at our emotions and force a response. It's why it continues to persist and thrive, even though we all know it exists.

It also taps into a more profound, longstanding cynicism that has always existed. Fake news might be a confection of its makers, but it latches onto (and grows thanks to) real issues that people have with authority. Sometimes, fake news thrives because of an absence of information; if we lack facts about something, our imaginations fill in the gaps. Other times, it's because the real answers provided aren't clear enough. Still other times, fake news capitalises on our desire to gossip – a human instinct that fosters bonding and social cohesion but also drives us to seek out and spread harmful information. Fake news is often presented in that 'need to know' way to make it seem more enticing – even when it's unbelievable.

So, don't scoff if you think people who believe fake news aren't like you. They are. And you'll likely have been taken in by it before. Instead, be aware of how it works and thrives – and be forewarned about how to stop it.

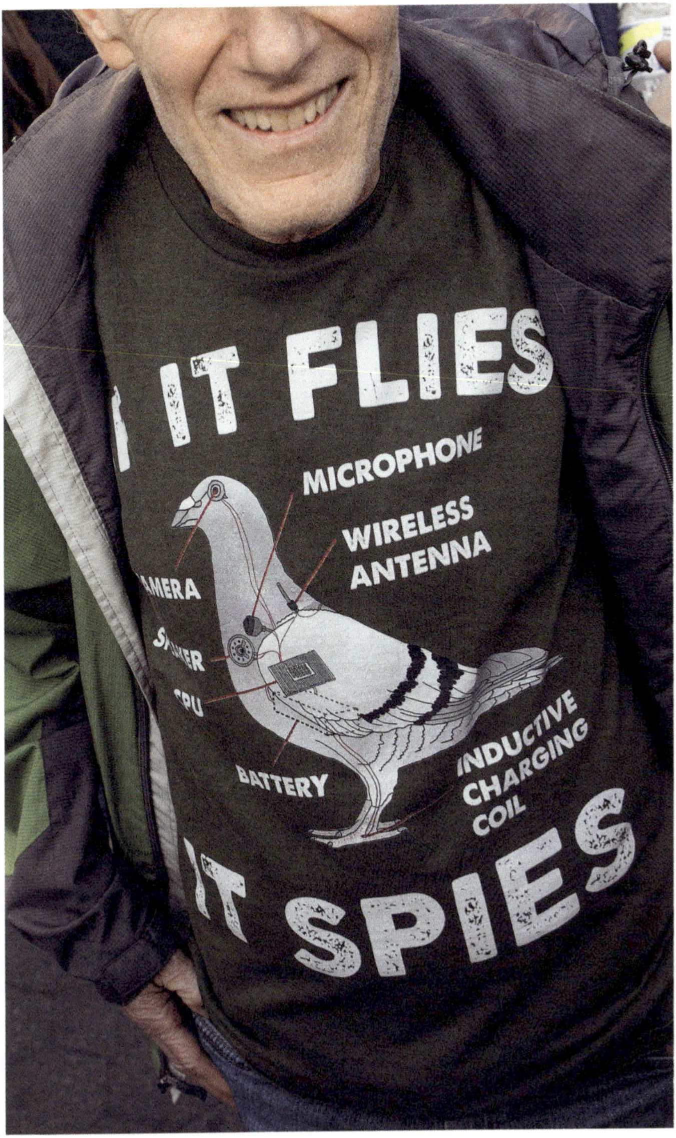
IT FLIES
MICROPHONE
WIRELESS
ANTENNA
BATTERY
INDUCTIVE
CHARGING
COIL
SPIES

How popular are conspiracy theories?

More common than you'd think. A 2021 survey by YouGov and the Cambridge Globalism Project saw researchers ask 25,000 people in 24 countries about their belief in 12 common conspiracy theories – from the Moon landings being faked to humans making contact with aliens. People in India were the most likely to believe conspiracies, with an average of 36 per cent believing each conspiracy was 'probably' or 'definitely' true. Other countries with high levels of belief included South Africa, Kenya, Nigeria and Thailand. But don't think this is just a problem in the Global South. Twenty per cent of American citizens and 13 per cent of Brits believe in conspiracies, as do one in five Australians and 16 per cent of Germans.

The way belief crosses borders suggests that something deeper is at play. Experiments have shown that when people feel anxious, they are more likely to think conspiratorially, perhaps to explain a threat that is hard to understand. This might be why fake news is a global phenomenon: it's a human response to a challenging world. The problem is that the anxiety-to-conspiracy path can quickly become a vicious cycle: the more people believe in conspiracies, the more anxious non-believers tend to become, which makes them, in turn, more susceptible to such beliefs.

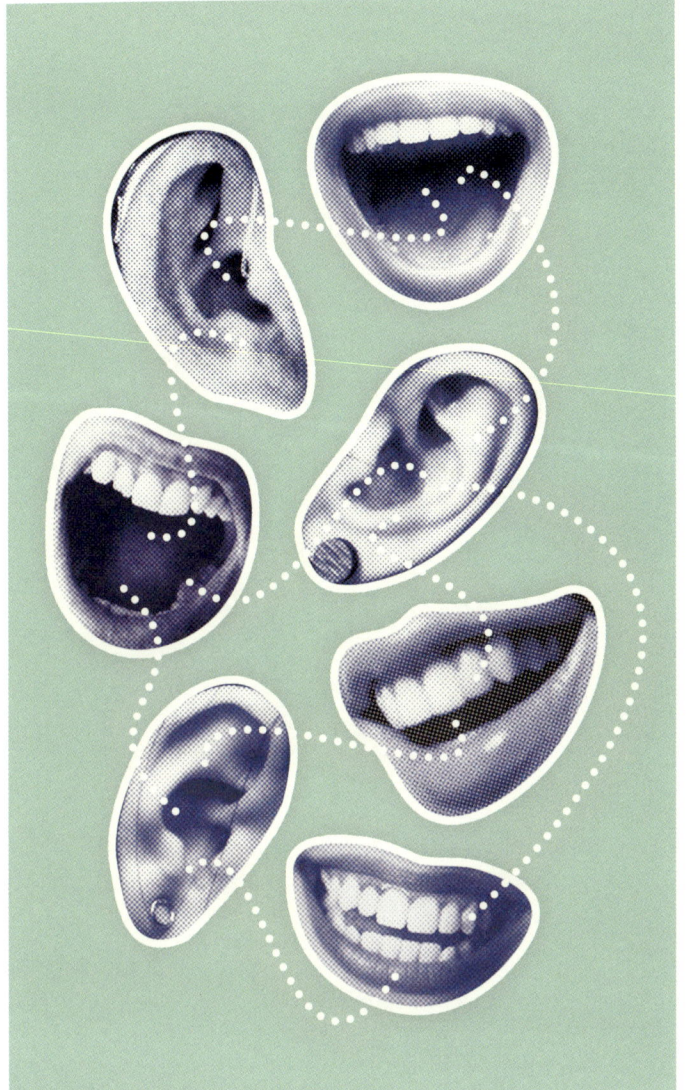

Graffiti on a wall in Michigan. 'Birds aren't real' – a deliberately incredulous claim that birds are actually government drones spying on citizens – is a popular satire of Donald Trump-inspired conspiracy theories.

Why does fake news matter?

It's a question that many people have: why do we make a song and dance about people's beliefs in outlandish theories – big or small? You're reading this book, so you might care more than the average person. But fake news matters not just because of the individual impact of each untruth being spread, but the compound impact it has. Every time someone spreads a lie, it weakens the belief in truth. Think of it like a wall of truth taking blows from a hammer: do it enough times, and the wall begins to crumble.

Humankind survives by believing others are acting in good faith. We tend to believe some people more than others; surveys show politicians, estate agents and journalists are often less believed than judges, police officers or nurses. However, if we reach a critical mass of fake news – whether real lies or accusations lobbed at truths – those standards of belief slip even further. Suddenly, we perceive a web of lies all around us. Day might be night. Up might be down. Truth might be fiction. Without trust in others' information, we can't be sure of anything outside our direct experience, and the world risks spiralling into madness. That's why fake news matters.

The long history of fake news

The history of rumour

Whether you're guessing who's the next big football transfer or sharing workplace gossip, rumour is a central part of human communication. And it always has been. According to evolutionary psychologist Robin Dunbar, it's baked into our development as a species: we gossip and spread rumours to maintain social networks, which were initially vital for our survival (and today remain important to staying sane).

While much of our day-to-day gossip is benign, history proves that spreading rumours can have seriously damaging consequences. In the 12th century, pogroms were carried out against Jews in England because of rumours that King Richard I had ordered violence against them. During the Salem Witch Trials of 1692, unfounded, scurrilous gossip led to the execution of innocent people. Invented in 1440, the printing press revolutionised the spread of ideas – and of rumours, propelling gossip into formal publications. Both World Wars saw governments' strategic use of rumour and propaganda to boost morale or demoralise the enemy.

Today, social media rumours are weaponised, using the speedy spread of public platforms to propel information around the world – whether true or not.

Fake news and democracy in Ancient Greece

Athens is known as the birthplace of democracy, but it was also a hotbed of fake news. Rumour and falsehoods were common currency in Ancient Greece, where political leaders often deployed fake news to damage opponents' reputations and gain public favour (sound familiar?). Public assemblies, agoras and symposia became breeding grounds for gossip, swaying public opinion.

The scandal of the Herms in 415 BCE is one such example. Overnight, herms (priapic statues of the god Hermes) that peppered Athens were vandalised, and the finger of blame pointed at Alcibiades, a prominent politician. Alcibiades was a social figure on the rise – which his opponents saw as dangerous. Linking him to the scandal was an easy way to neutralise his power. The claims were unsubstantiated, but Alcibiades suffered, eventually being tried and losing his position. Gossip and fake news were used to undermine political rivals – setting the scene for thousands of years in the future.

Socrates chides his pupil Alcibiades. Alcibiades was later the victim of
the Scandal of Herms, when he was falsely accused of vandalising statues
of the god Hermes and suffered reputational damage as a result.

Sir Francis Bacon in his parliamentary robes. The philosopher,
statesman and author described an early account of
confirmation bias in his work *Novum Organum*.

Francis Bacon and the origins of confirmation bias

Confirmation bias is one of the ways that fake news can spread. This bias involves paying more attention to evidence that supports our existing beliefs. Frankly, life is less painful when we believe we're right. But when we only encounter information we agree with, it helps silo us into so-called 'filter bubbles'. The phenomenon is especially present on social media, where algorithms determine what we see, but the idea has a surprisingly long history.

Francis Bacon, one of the Enlightenment's main figures, described the idea in his philosophical work *Novum Organum*, published in 1620. Bacon pinpointed several 'idols', sources of error that cloud human judgment, including one that he dubbed the 'Idols of the Tribe'. (Bacon used the term 'idols' because he felt belief in them was similar to belief in objects or individuals of misguided worship – or 'false idols'.) Bacon warned of an issue that we now know all too well: people often accept evidence that aligns with their views while disregarding contradictory information, even if it's factually correct – leading to flawed conclusions and impeding scientific progress (conspiracists who believe cellular technology is harming our health were quick to point out that there were 5G towers installed in Wuhan before the Covid-19 outbreak, for example).

Jean Hardouin, a French priest and scholar best known
for his unorthodox conspiracy theories.

The first-ever conspiracy theory?

It's tempting to view conspiracy theorists as a blight specific to the digital age, but this is a misconception. In 1693, priest Jean Hardouin proposed an unusual idea that some consider the first-ever conspiracy theory.

Hardouin suggested that almost all the classical literature we've been given – centuries of writing by some of the world's most recognisable authors – wasn't created by them and wasn't created at that time. Instead, he argued that a handful of monks and scholars came together in the 13th century to rewrite history, forging documents to better support their beliefs. Hardouin was sceptical of the source of classical literature because he worried it could undercut wider belief in religion.

The claims were as explosive as they were shaky. Hardouin relied on analysis of the language used to support his idea of a grand forgery, suggesting that some texts were filled with anachronisms that didn't exist when they were meant to be written. His analysis was treated with scepticism by many (one contemporary described him as 'violently addicted to hypothesis and paradox'). Still, it was trusted by some and demonstrated a tactic that would become more prevalent in the centuries to come: dismissing things you disagree with as conspiracies and forgeries.

Artificial intelligence in the 18th century

The Mechanical Turk, developed in the 18th century by Hungarian inventor Wolfgang von Kempelen, was an elaborate, autonomous chess-playing machine that duped and captivated the royal courts of Europe for decades. The machine consisted of a life-sized mechanical figure in Ottoman robes seated at a wooden cabinet. It also possessed the finest chess mind in the world, defeating all opponents, including Napoleon Bonaparte and Benjamin Franklin.

Some argued that the Mechanical Turk was one of the world's first artificial intelligences. But the reality is more prosaic: the Turk's grand robes concealed a human chess player inside its cabinet, making the moves. It is an early example of fake news and gullibility intertwining, alongside a heavy dose of starry-eyed tech hype. Despite being exposed in the early 19th century, the Mechanical Turk continued to tour and mystify audiences, illustrating a key facet of fake news: our willingness to believe the unbelievable.

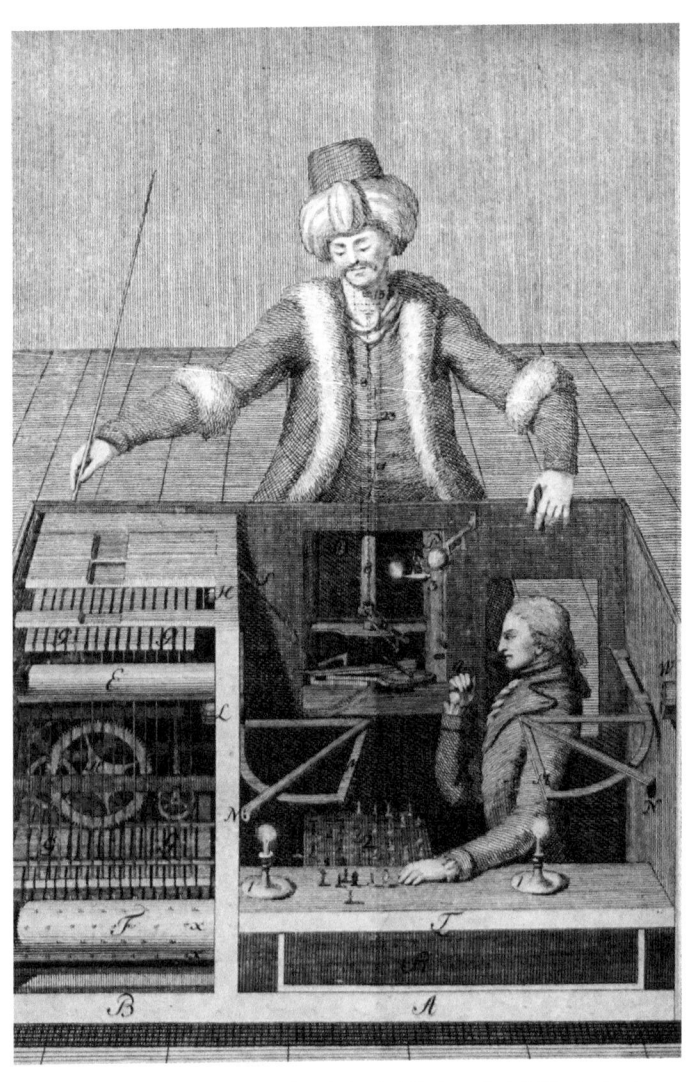

An engraving shows how the Mechanical Turk worked. A life-sized constructed figure appeared to be playing chess autonomously; in fact, a human was making the moves, hidden from within a cabinet.

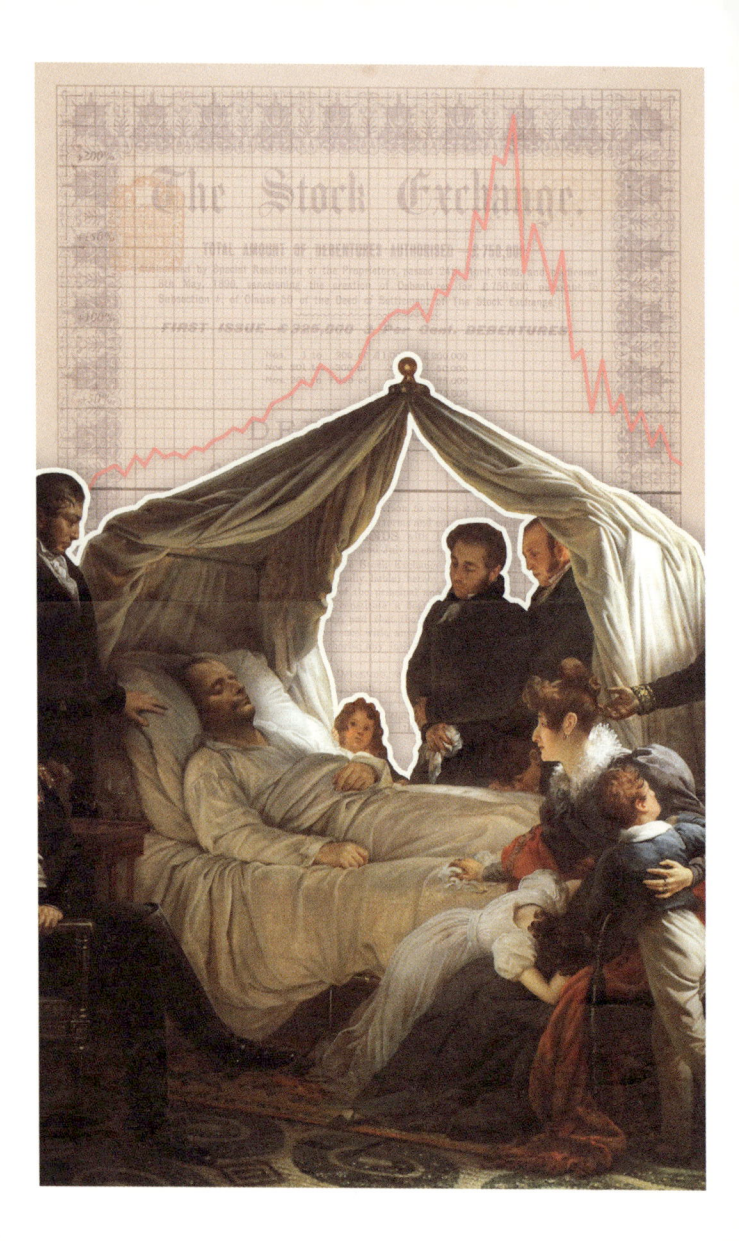

The fake death of Napoleon

Major news can move financial markets – whether it's real or not. One February morning in 1814, two men in resplendent uniforms turned up at an inn in Dover, bringing news of the death of Napoleon, the French emperor. The leader of the duo, who called himself Colonel du Bourg, said the emperor had been killed during his war-waging, and Bourbon rule had been re-established in France.

There was just one problem: Napoleon would live for seven more years. And he definitely remained in charge. Still, news travelled quickly, aided by du Bourg stopping off at several other inns on his way to London.

Word got through to London's stock traders, and the likelihood that allies would win the war bolstered markets, pushing the price of British government securities higher as £1.1 million of government-based stocks (over £74 million in today's money) were traded on a single day. That was good news for the people who bought them the week before.

It turned out to be an attempt by eight people, including an MP, to manipulate the markets, and they were convicted of conspiracy to defraud.

Fake news in the mass media

The Great Moon Hoax

In August 1835, readers of *The New York Sun* were enchanted by out-of-this-world news – literally. A series of six front-page articles announced the discovery of life on the Moon, captivating readers with tales of lunar cities, unicorns and bat-like humanoids. Known retrospectively as the Great Moon Hoax, these sensational stories – allegedly based on observations by British astronomer Sir John Herschel (son of the man who discovered Uranus) – described vivacious lunar landscapes populated by exotic creatures.

The series of stories was supposedly satire written by reporter Richard Adams Locke, but many readers took them as genuine. After all, it was printed in the newspaper, and most people knew little better about the Moon. *The Sun*'s circulation soared above average as people devoured the fantastical accounts. However, the truth soon emerged on the pages of *The Sun* itself a month later: the stories were fabrications. But the Great Moon Hoax highlights an early example of media sensationalism and marks the beginning of a period in which the authority of mainstream news outlets was increasingly challenged.

Illustrations from the *New York Sun* depicting some of
the creatures allegedly living on the Moon. The text reads,
'Discoveries made in the moon by Mr Herschell' [sic] – a British
astronomer to whom the discoveries were falsely attributed.

A *Puck* cartoon from 1888 satirises the evil spirits of the modern daily press, including 'paid puffery', 'suggestiveness' and 'scandal' – all key features of so-called yellow journalism.

How yellow journalism brought about war

Newspapers today like to lay claim to election victories or winning public interest campaigns and changing laws. They're less keen to bring about war. Yet that's what so-called yellow journalism did to the Spanish-American War in 1898.

Emerging from a battle for readers between two New York newspapers in the 1890s, the 'yellow press' was named for a popular comic strip – the 'Yellow Kid' – that appeared in both the *New York Journal* and the *New York World* during the circulation war. The papers focused on salacious scandal and violence, using exaggerated headlines and unverified claims to sell more copies. This included upping the ante in their reporting on Cubans' struggle to win independence from Spain, with missives that became ever more lurid, painting the Spaniards as brutal oppressors. When the USS Maine exploded in Havana Harbour, killing 266 American sailors, yellow journalists were quick to blame Spain, although there wasn't hard evidence.

The coverage prompted the US government to declare war on the Spanish on 25 April 1898. Hundreds of thousands of Americans fought in the war, and 2,000 died. And the yellow journalism that caused the war doesn't seem far away from today's clickbait headlines and mawkish revelations.

The Jewish Peril

PROTOCOLS

OF THE

Learned Elders

of Zion.

SECOND EDITION.

Published by "THE BRITONS," 62 Oxford Street, London, W.

1920.

Price. 3/- Net.

An early English edition of the *Protocols of the Elders of Zion*, a fabricated text supposedly describing a Jewish plot for world domination. The text has been described as 'probably the most influential work of antisemitism ever written'.

The document that launched an international Jewish conspiracy

The fatal flaw of fake news is that, no matter how false, stories are sometimes considered legitimate if they chime with people's beliefs (p.23). So it is with the *Protocols of the Elders of Zion*, one of the most notorious and enduring works of antisemitic propaganda. Purporting to be the minutes of a secret meeting of Jewish leaders plotting global domination, the document, first published in 1903, was a total fabrication.

Originating in Russia, the document was conjured up by elements within the Tsarist secret police to incite anti-semitism and bolster support for the autocratic regime. Anti-Bolshevik Russian emigrés spread the *Protocols* to the West in 1917, and editions soon appeared across the world. The claims were debunked in the 1920s, but it didn't matter to many – including the Nazis, who used the *Protocols* to justify persecution and violence against Jews during World War II.

Today, the *Protocols* continues to feed antisemitic sentiments worldwide, inspiring political speeches, editorials and even television programmes. The fact that it was discredited over 100 years ago doesn't stop it from being distributed widely online by those looking to spread hate.

The Cottingley Fairies

In the age of Photoshop, we are all well-versed in doubting the validity of certain imagery – but in 1917, photographs were considered more authoritative. So it was significant when cousins Elsie Wright and Frances Griffiths apparently captured images of fairies at the bottom of Griffiths' garden in Cottingley, England, in June of that year. The photos, showing Griffiths with fairies dancing in the foreground, were taken to convince their parents of their fantastical encounters.

They gained a far greater audience when Arthur Conan Doyle, the creator of Sherlock Holmes and a spiritualist enthusiast, published them in a 1920 article, citing the photos as proof of supernatural life. Doyle's article sold out within days of publication, though generally, press coverage was sceptical.

It took until the 1980s for Wright and Griffiths to admit the images were faked, created by cutting out illustrations from a popular children's book and posing these in conspicuous places. 'I never even thought of it as being a fraud,' explained Frances in a 1985 interview with Yorkshire Television. 'I can't understand to this day why [people] were taken in – they wanted to be taken in.' Not only is this one of the earliest examples of photographic fake news, but it is also a powerful lesson in why we're susceptible to it; after all, who wouldn't want to believe there are fairies at the bottom of the garden?

One of the infamous photographs demonstrating the existence of the Cottingley Fairies, published by Arthur Conan Doyle in a 1920 article.

The 'Uncle Sam: I Want You for U.S. Army' poster was produced in 1917. The poster was used to recruit soldiers into the US Army in both World War I and World War II.

World War I, propaganda and PR

No population wants war – which is why propaganda is so important in selling it to the masses. World War I was the first conflict that saw governments across Europe and the United States methodically produce propaganda. They employed vivid imagery and emotive slogans to inspire patriotism and encourage enlistment, perpetuating a narrative of 'us' versus 'them'.

Iconic images, such as the British 'Lord Kitchener Wants You' poster, first printed in 1914, and the American 'Uncle Sam: I Want You for U.S. Army' poster from 1917, where the fictional figure points directly at the viewer, became powerful symbols of national unity and resolve. The emotional nature of the posters tapped into public fears of invading forces – as well as a sense of duty – convincing many to sign up against their better judgement.

Edward Bernays, a propagandist at the US Committee on Public Information during World War I, realised that these enormously successful tactics had application away from the battlefield. In 1928, he published a book called *Propaganda*, arguing that the same principles of mass psychology could manipulate the public via advertising campaigns, birthing a whole new industry: PR.

The controversial
Leni Riefenstahl

Propaganda – information designed to influence public opinion – often masquerades as something else. Sometimes, the political agenda is so covert that we don't realise we are being influenced at all. Leni Riefenstahl, a pioneering German filmmaker, remains a controversial figure due to her role in producing Nazi propaganda – which many consider an early form of fake news. Her most famous film, *Triumph of the Will* (1935), documented the 1934 Nuremberg Rally, showcasing Adolf Hitler and the National Socialist movement with striking cinematography and something of a God complex. The film was lauded for its artistic skill but lambasted for its subtle glorification of Nazi ideology via Riefenstahl's dramatic camera angles and revolutionary use of music.

After the fall of the Nazis and until her death in 2003, Riefenstahl claimed to be an apolitical artist who was merely documenting events. But critics say her work significantly legitimised and amplified Hitler's regime. Writing in 1975, Susan Sontag noted that Riefenstahl was even involved in orchestrating the rally, treating it as a movie set for her film. 'In *Triumph of the Will*, the document (the image) is no longer simply the record of reality; "reality" has been constructed to serve the image,' Sontag wrote.

Filmmaker Leni Riefenstahl on the set of *Triumph of the Will* (1935). Riefenstahl insisted she was an apolitical documentarian, but critics argue that she was a Nazi propagandist (and indeed, the party funded several of her films).

The radio hoax that caused public panic

The Houses of Parliament had been destroyed. Big Ben had been laid to waste. That was the message of a live BBC radio report delivered to listeners on 16 January 1926 by Father Ronald Knox under the title *Broadcasting the Barricades*.

Concussion shells punctuated live music as it was broadcast over the airwaves, and listeners began to fear their country was at war again. What was behind it wasn't certain, but the country was already in turmoil over labour disputes, so people took it seriously.

They weren't meant to. It was a comedic skit – the names of characters, including Sir Theophilus Gooch and Miss Joy Gush, were meant to hint at that. But not everyone got the joke. The BBC received complaints from 249 listeners (although it's worth noting that 2,307 people wrote in to say they enjoyed the prank). Nevertheless, the broadcaster was chastened. The incident gave a sense of their responsibilities – and, some would argue, turned the BBC po-faced in its seriousness. Still, it could poke fun, as we'll see elsewhere in this book.

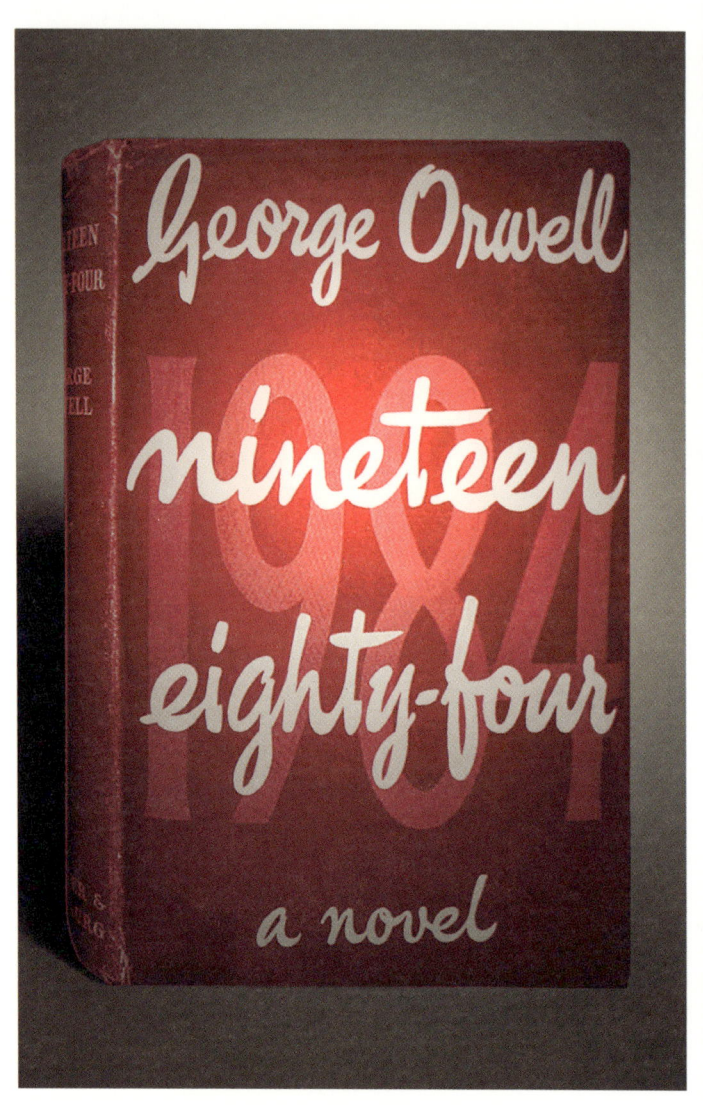

The first edition of George Orwell's *Nineteen Eighty-Four*, published in 1949.

George Orwell's visionary novel

Since its release in 1949, George Orwell's novel *Nineteen Eighty-Four* has become a byword for government surveillance and lies. In the book, the ruling party seeks to rewrite history to support its goals in power – pushing fake news on the populace through the so-called Ministry of Truth. The manipulation of truth goes beyond changing facts: it also alters language itself, with Newspeak – which has a deliberately limited vocabulary – intended to put a throttle on free thought.

Orwell was ahead of his time forecasting the impact of 'doublethink' – the ability to hold two contradictory beliefs and accept them as true. The psychological toll of these conflicting 'realities' is something we struggle with today (just look at those who accuse migrants of somehow stealing their jobs *and* their benefits, or others who insist that wars are fought for peace).

Ironically, although Orwell forewarned of a totalitarian regime led by Big Brother in which the very nature of truth was undermined, his work has become a *cause célèbre* for those who believe in fake news. Supporters of Donald Trump and others peddling falsehoods are often the first to accuse government institutions of Orwellian surveillance.

A Soviet propaganda poster titled 'The Culture of Capitalism' (1952). The term *dezinformatsiya* first appeared in print in 1952, used by the Soviets to describe tactics they believed their Western opponents were employing.

The Soviet origins of disinformation

The slightly swottier way to describe fake news is 'disinformation', which comes from the Russian word *dezinformatsiya*. History suggests that Stalin invented the word after World War II. Indeed, it appeared in the 1952 edition of the *Great Soviet Encyclopaedia*, which describes it as 'dissemination (in the press, on the radio, etc.) of false reports intended to mislead public opinion'. Curiously, the word was being used to describe underhand tactics that Soviet overlords believed their Western opponents were employing… but it was Soviet spies who put the disinformation playbook into action.

From planting fake stories in media outlets to circulating forged documents and manipulating photos, Soviet operatives spun a web of lies and half-truths designed to cloak reality. Their methods ranged from the crude – such as spreading rumours that the CIA invented AIDS – to the sublime, such as funding Western peace groups to subtly broadcast Soviet messaging. And while the Soviet Union ceased to exist as of 1991, Russian supremacy in the disinformation space lives on, sowing uncertainty today – most obviously in the 2016 US election.

Stalin's primitive 'Photoshopping'

Photo manipulation had been going on long before Photoshop was launched – as Joseph Stalin could attest. Stalin's Soviet regime (1924–1953) frequently altered photographs to erase political enemies and create an idealised image of Soviet leadership. The practice involved manually editing images using techniques like retouching, airbrushing and compositing (combining two images) – all skills that are now relatively easy to achieve through Photoshop.

One of the most famous examples of Stalin's primitive – or should that be *prototypical* – Photoshopping saw Nikolai Yezhov, the former head of the NKVD (Soviet secret police), removed from photographs after his execution in 1938. This iconic photograph shows Stalin walking along the Moscow-Volga Canal with Soviet premier Vyacheslav Molotov on his right shoulder and Yezhov on his left shoulder. But after Yezhov's execution, he magically disappeared from all official copies of the photograph.

Spot the difference. The first image shows Stalin with Nikolai Yezhov – former head of the Soviet secret police – on his left shoulder. Following Yezhov's execution for his 'anti-Soviet' conduct during the Great Purge, Stalin had the image doctored to remove all evidence of him.

A still from the BBC's 1957 *Panorama* broadcast supposedly
showing people in Switzerland harvesting spaghetti from trees.

The Swiss spaghetti harvest

Viewers switching on their television sets to watch the BBC's *Panorama* current affairs programme on 1 April 1957 were confronted with an incredible story. Richard Dimbleby, one of the country's most trusted and beloved broadcasters, narrated a report from the Swiss region of Ticino. Farmers in the country were expecting a bumper harvest of spaghetti from trees that year, thanks to a mild winter and victory in the war against dreaded grain-eating pests.

Some context is important: back then, pasta was not as common a meal on Britons' dinner plates as it is today. And the fact that the BBC – the country's national broadcaster – was devoting so much time (three minutes) to the story gave it legitimacy. Dimbleby's dry demeanour while presenting the report also helped make a convincing case. Eagle-eyed viewers noticed something was up when they looked at the date it was broadcast. It was an early April Fool's Day prank – but one that tricked large swathes of the watching public, showing what happens when you combine public ignorance of a topic with the authority of a legitimate news brand.

Man on the Moon (or not)

One small step for man was a giant leap too far for a fifth of Americans today, who believe the 1969 Moon landing was faked. This isn't a new belief: books and documents in the 1970s, following up on claims made by aerospace contractor Bill Kaysing, suggested that what was seen as the surface of the Moon was, in fact, a sound stage firmly back on Earth. Why does the theory convince so many? The near-50-year wait between the Apollo missions and the current Artemis missions doesn't help quell conspiracies.

The lunar landing conspiracy theory is an early example of fake news taking hold among a significant proportion of the population long before the widespread advent of the internet. And while this was an analogue conspiracy theory when it was conceived, the internet may have given it a second life. Interestingly, Moon hoaxism is more prevalent among those aged 24–35 (21 per cent believed the landing was staged) than it is among over-55s (just 13 per cent agreed). As the number of witnesses who watched the landing on TV in 1969 decreases with time, and theories proliferate on platforms like YouTube and Reddit, the Moon landing conspiracy seems only to get stronger.

Apollo 11 astronaut Buzz Aldrin walks on the Moon, 1969. Conspiracists suggested that what appears to be the surface of the Moon was actually a stage set.

Aliens in the desert

Misinformation thrives in a vacuum or amid confusion. Want proof? Look no further than the Roswell incident, which remains one of the most enduring conspiracy theories in human history.

Here are the facts: in 1947, a US Air Force balloon crashed near Roswell, New Mexico. Initial reports from the organisation misdescribed it as a 'flying disc', which made international headlines before it was retracted a day later, with the Army claiming it was a weather balloon.

From there, conspiracy theories took hold, fuelled by military reticence to reveal exactly what was going on in and around Roswell, a key location for research and development of new technologies. In 1978, a US Air Force officer said the weather balloon explanation was a red herring, adding more fuel to the sceptical fire. In the 1990s, it was revealed the balloon involved was part of a project to detect nuclear testing, but for decades, the government and military had kept schtum.

There's no evidence whatsoever that a UFO full of aliens crashed on that day in 1947 (and plenty of evidence to the contrary). But for those who want to believe, it's a major moment in alien–earthling relations – belief in which still lives on today. Why? Because sometimes the scarier idea is the notion that we are utterly alone in the universe after all.

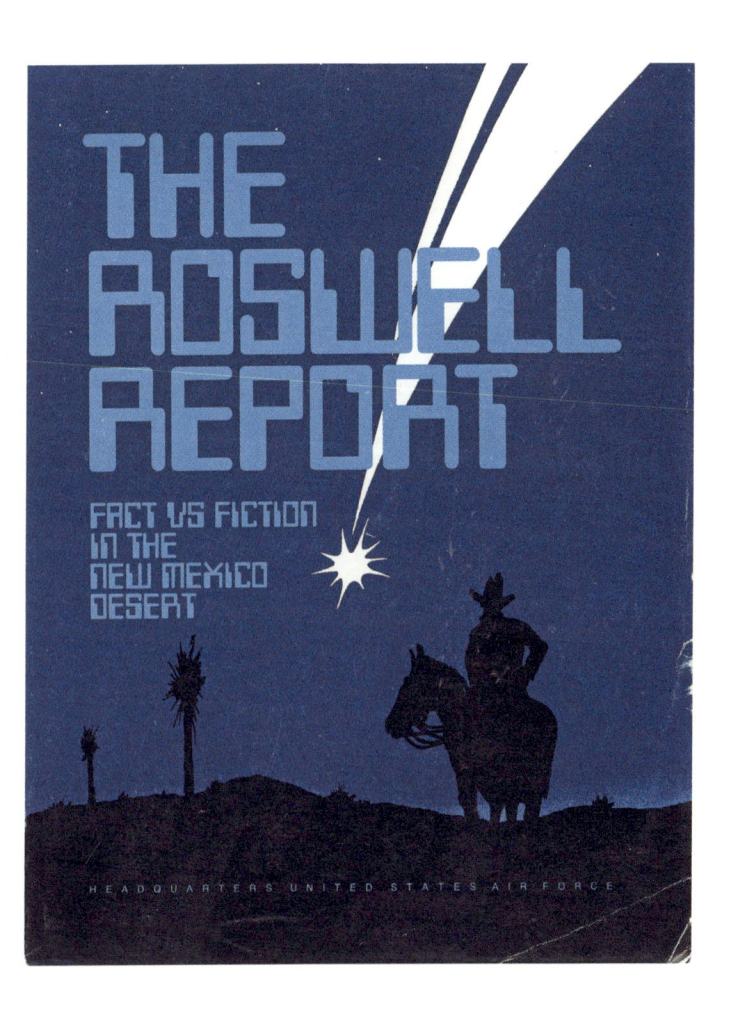

THE ROSWELL REPORT

FACT VS FICTION IN THE NEW MEXICO DESERT

HEADQUARTERS UNITED STATES AIR FORCE

In 1995, the US Air Force published this official response to the Roswell Incident, admitting that the weather balloon story was a cover-up for a nuclear testing programme. They hoped to debunk the conspiracy, but polls from the time show that the majority of Americans doubted the explanation.

The War Against Naked Animals

He Aims to Put Pants On Dogs, Slips on Horses And Even Bikinis on Cows!

By BERNARD HENRY

G. Clifford Prout has declared war on naked animals.

As President of the Society for Indecency to Naked Animals — known as SINA — Prout has dedicated 10 years of his life to clothing the "vital areas" of animals.

He wants dogs to wear pants and horses to wear half slips.

He's designed bikinis for cows and even trousers for elephants. "It's a matter of decency," Prout explained. "Naked animals are ruining the moral standards of America."

Prout began his campaign against unclothed animals in 1906, when he received $400,000 in his father's will.

The money had to be spent within 10 years, according to

Prout believes that all animals have a built-in sense of modesty and that they prefer to wear clothes.

"People who don't clothe their animals are at fault," he said.

Whenever Prout hears about a case of animal nudity, he sends a letter to the offending person. In 1959 he wrote to Northwest Orient Airlines complaining about a naked horse in the company's show window in New York.

Last June he sent a letter to David Sarnoff, board chairman of RCA, pointing out that the RCA trademark — a dog called Nipper — way immodest.

Besides the mail campaign,

BAMBI COVERS UP: Deer's vital areas have been covered up to the satisfaction of G. Clifford Prout, president and founder of the Society for Indecency to Naked Animals.

A well-known prankster, Alan Abel founded the Society for Indecency to Naked Animals (SINA) in 1959, campaigning to clothe all animals to preserve their dignity.

Alan Abel, American prankster

Alan Abel's place of birth – Zanesville, Ohio – feels fitting for a man best known for his outlandish hoaxes. And in 1980, Abel made his most outlandish hoax yet. Abel decided to try and hoodwink the world by faking his death, organising an obituary to be published in the *New York Times* that suggested he had died of a heart attack while skiing in Utah. A fake funeral director collected his belongings, and a woman posing as his widow notified the paper.

A day after the *New York Times* obituary was published, Abel called a press conference, where he 'returned from the dead'. His was the first obituary to be retracted in *New York Times* history.

In hindsight, journalists should have been sceptical. Abel was well-known for convincing the media to cover his over-the-top stunts, including a 1959 movement to make the Society for Indecency to Naked Animals, or SINA, a mass movement. SINA wanted to clothe all animals to return dignity to their existence and to prevent the humans that encountered them from being offended. Sometimes, the impetus behind fake news is not malice but good old-fashioned mischief.

Hitler's diaries

It was the find of a lifetime. Sixty volumes of diaries penned by Adolf Hitler were discovered in a hayloft in 1983 and brought to the market by an antiques dealer named Konrad Fischer. No wonder German magazine *Stern* was willing to pay $3.7 million for the diaries and sold the rights to several other publications – including the UK's *Sunday Times*.

There was an issue, however: Konrad Fischer was Konrad Kujau, a serial forger. Rather than being written by Hitler, the diaries were put together by Kujau over two years, between 1981 and 1983. Kujau had practised writing in old German gothic script for a month and sprinkled the pages with tea to give them an aged look. The diaries mostly contained lists of Nazi party promotions and official engagements – information taken from history books about Hitler's day-to-day activities.

Historians were ambivalent about whether the work was legitimate – for good reason. The fakes were quickly exposed by forensic examination. Heads rolled at the newspapers, and Kujau went to prison.

The incident dealt a blow to what had, until then, been considered a paper of great renown, showing how easy it was to manipulate the news.

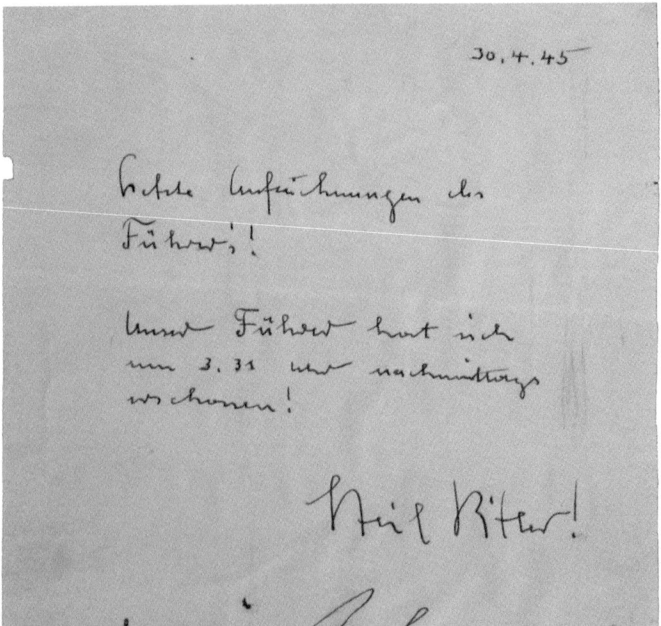

[Handwritten note in German, largely illegible:]

Letzte Aufzeichnungen des
Führers!

Unser Führer hat sich
um 3.31 Uhr nachmittags
erschossen!

Heil Hitler!

Martin Bormann.
Dr. Goebbels.

The last circulating copy of the fake Hitler diaries, pictured above,
was auctioned to an anonymous bidder for €6,500 in 2004.

A 1907 anti-vaccination caricature shows a doctor, surrounded by quack medical treatments, vaccinating a patient against smallpox by poking holes in their face.

The MMR vaccine scare

Andrew Wakefield's 1998 study in *The Lancet* was like many others that the medical journal published: prosaic, impenetrable and supported by supposed evidence. But the study was *unlike* many others because of its impact. Wakefield claimed a link between the MMR (measles, mumps and rubella) vaccine and autism, sparking widespread fear and huge scepticism towards vaccination that would persist for decades to come. The proportion of British children vaccinated against MMR dropped from around 91 per cent in the mid-1990s to 80 per cent by the mid-2000s.

There were issues with Wakefield's study, though. It was based on only 12 cases and suggested that the combined vaccine triggered bowel disease, leading to developmental disorders. Some say Wakefield was also corrupted by financial conflicts of interest and guilty of manipulating data. In 2010, *The Lancet* retracted the paper, and Wakefield was stripped of his medical license. Subsequent studies unequivocally found no link between the MMR vaccine and autism.

Yet the theories cut through, aided by the press, who persisted in publishing the findings even after the study was retracted. It took two decades for vaccination levels to return to where they were before Wakefield's paper. And even now, some still believe Wakefield was right.

The digital age

Terry Pratchett's prediction

Since the early days of the internet, there have been concerns about what this great leveller in communication hierarchy could do to the truth. Some of those concerns came from an unusual place: fantasy novelist Terry Pratchett, who, in a 1995 interview with Microsoft founder Bill Gates, worried about conspiracy theories and fake news.

'Let's say I call myself the Institute for Something-or-other and I decide to promote a spurious treatise saying the Jews were entirely responsible for the Second World War and the Holocaust didn't happen,' Pratchett said. 'And it goes out there on the internet and is available on the same terms as any piece of historical research which has undergone peer review [...] There's no way of finding out whether this stuff has any bottom to it or whether someone has just made it up.' The fear proved eerily prescient. Gates, at the time, said it wouldn't be likely. But fantasy became reality, and what some saw as an overly dramatic prediction arguably understated the real impact.

Why social media breeds fake news

Fake news has existed long before the advent of social media. Yet platforms on which we share memories, thoughts and news have helped supercharge the spread of disinformation. Why?

The answer is complicated, but it comes down to several factors. One factor is the thing that makes social media so brilliant: the levelling of authority. It removes the gatekeepers that prevent alternative viewpoints being heard. But without the hierarchy of traditional media, there's no one fact-checking these viewpoints either.

Content goes viral by sparking strong emotions in us. Social media platforms are deliberately designed to make it easy to share outrage quickly – before we think about why and how our buttons are being pressed.

People have always spread harmful gossip, but historically, the impact of this has been limited by the physical size of our social groups; there are only so many people you can whisper a secret to. Social media changes that, allowing us to spread information through far-reaching and often tenuous connections. As a result, secrets can reach millions in a matter of seconds.

Echo chambers and algorithms

Everyone in your Instagram feed shares the same infographics and likes the same memes. That funny video you sent a friend? They've already seen it. The algorithms that power social media platforms play a crucial role in forming echo chambers – where a person only encounters views that mirror their own. Designed to maximise user engagement, social media algorithms track our interactions and preferences, showing us more content we will likely engage with. This can mean more articles, videos and posts that align with our preexisting beliefs and fewer that challenge them. As a result, our worldview becomes increasingly narrow, and our opinions are continuously reinforced.

This phenomenon makes the spread of fake news particularly insidious. When misinformation is shared within an echo chamber, it gains credibility simply because it is repeated and endorsed by others within the same bubble. The more it's shared, the more it appears legitimate. This self-reinforcing cycle makes it extremely difficult for outside information, even if factual, to penetrate and correct the false narratives being perpetuated. Try to puncture the filter bubble (as it's also known), and you're considered an enemy – and often accused of peddling fake news yourself.

Clickbait: yellow journalism for the digital age

You won't BELIEVE what the media industry does to drive visitors to its website. There's ONE AMAZING TRICK that can help news websites garner vast internet traffic.

And you've just encountered it: clickbait is rife and well. It involves amping up the content of a news story to try and encourage a reader to click on it – an important skill in a digital world where the average person is drowning under endless other distractions, and you're seeking to raise your content above the morass on social media.

Yet amping up can quickly become overegging. Bridging what's called the 'curiosity gap' – giving enough information to entice a reader to click while not directly answering the question posed – can quickly become misleading. Seen as a new iteration of yellow journalism (p.35), editor-in-chief of the *Guardian*, Katharine Viner, has lamented clickbait as 'chasing down cheap clicks at the expense of accuracy and veracity'.

East London
You WON'T BELIEVE what Martin Usborne spotted this FOX doing...

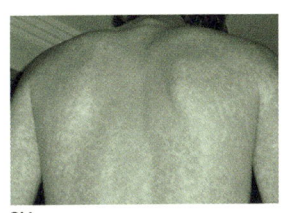

Skincare
Dermatologists HATE this one little skincare tip...

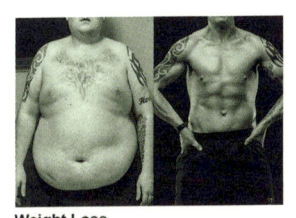

Weight Loss
One Kansas man's INCREDIBLE weight loss journey...

Music
No one expected THIS to happen to Beatles STAR in 1966...

Supermarkets
What the big supermarkets AREN'T telling you about their produce...

Media
How a media group PERFECTED the secret to online engagement...

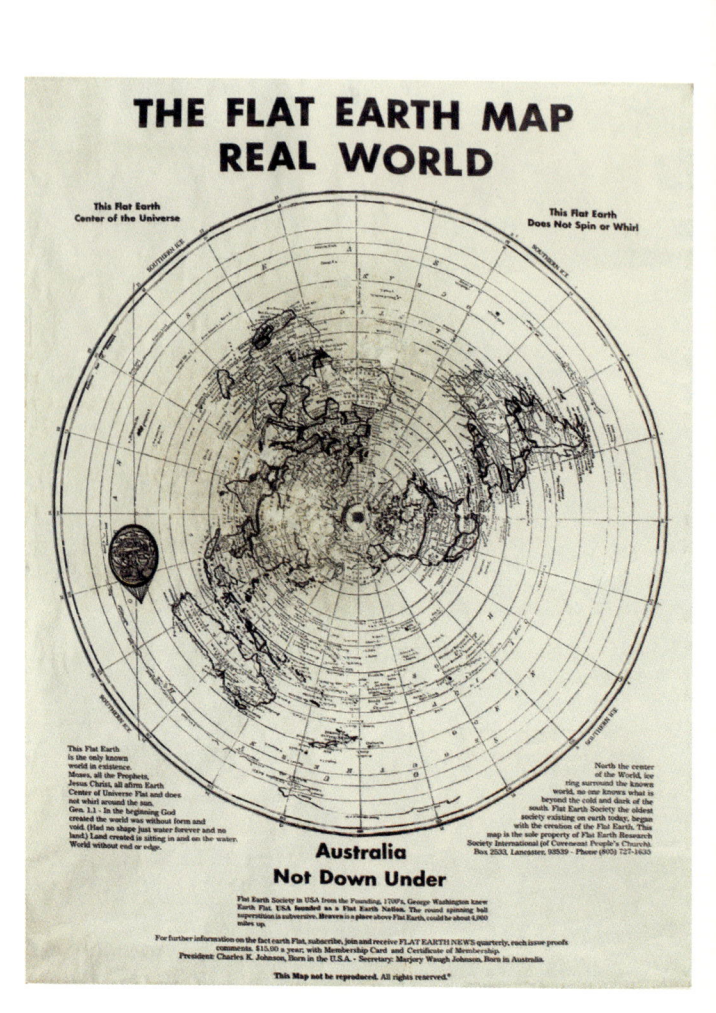

A 20th-century map published by the Flat Earth Society.

Who really believes the Earth is flat?

Set sail in a straight line from any point in the world, and eventually, you'll end up back where you began. It's a simple fact taught to children in geography lessons. But not everyone believes it. In fact, one in ten Americans believe the Earth is flat, including NBA basketball player Kyrie Irving and rapper B.o.B, who even released a diss track aimed at physicist Neil deGrasse Tyson.

Of course, the belief was widely held several hundred years ago. Although ideas of the Earth's spherical shape date back to Ancient Greece, most ordinary people from Antiquity through to the Middle Ages couldn't read and hadn't travelled, so their understanding of the planet and its place in the universe was limited. This changed in the 17th century with the Copernican Revolution and Isaac Newton's writings. By 1849, when writer Samuel Rowbotham published a flat Earth pamphlet (spawning the modern conspiracy), people really should have known better.

In the digital age, these theories attract those who are distrustful of authority. It's not *just* that the planet is flat; it's that there's a grand government cover-up designed to quell free thought. If they're lying about something as fundamental as the shape of our planet, the conspiracist argument goes, what else are they lying about?

How a freak child snatching turned out to be fake

Golden eagles aren't normally seen in and around Montreal, Canada – which was the first hint that all was not right when a video of one such bird appeared on YouTube in December 2012. The next clue that something was amiss: the eagle swept down over Mount Royal Park, used its talons to hoist a toddler from the grass, and carried them for a few feet before dropping them.

News reporters were agog at the threat posed to humanity. The video became a must-watch, clocking up 17 million views within the first 24 hours of being posted.

But there was one problem: it was a sham. It was the work of four students in a video-effects class at a technology university in Montreal. The lecturer running the class, Robin Tremblay, had set an assignment for his students: make a viral hoax video. The students got an A if the video got more than 100,000 views. Needless to say, they got the top grade. This was one of the earliest internet-powered fake news videos – and only the beginning.

A still from the 1908 silent film *Rescued from an Eagle's Nest* – another (much older) story concerning a baby being abducted by an eagle The rudimentary special effects involved a stuffed bird, operated by wires, and a real baby set against a moving painted backdrop.

What makes something go viral?

Anyone can make up a story. But when does a made-up story become fake news? It's partly due to how many people it affects. If fake news is false stories sent into orbit, then virality is the engine that propels them there.

Virality online refers to the phenomenon where content is shared by a large number of people, rapidly gaining widespread attention. Once that sharing reaches a critical mass, virality has a life of its own. It can shoot into the stratosphere, breaking orbit... or it can fizzle out in the atmosphere, stall and crash back down to Earth.

Virality is built up in several ways, but it comes down to pushing people's buttons. Sometimes, it's content that's too funny not to share with friends. Sometimes, outrage motivates sharing, such as the video of a golden eagle snatching a child (p.76). Bad actors use both tactics to disseminate disinformation by getting you to press share before you think about why you're doing it. Off the back of that, viral content is born, and fake news takes flight.

The Sandy Hook conspiracy

Fake news can cause real harm, as the families of victims of the Sandy Hook school shooting know all too well. On 14 December 2012, a mass shooter killed 26 people at Sandy Hook Elementary. Families of murdered children faced a second indignity: conspiracy theorists latched onto the shooting, suggesting it was a hoax created by the government to implement stricter gun control laws. Others suggested, incorrectly, that the victims' families were 'crisis actors' and that no children had died.

Many of the conspiracy theories were spearheaded by Alex Jones, whose online news show Infowars poured fire on the flames. Victims and their families faced harassment, threats and accusations from conspiracy believers, compounding their suffering. Legal action was eventually taken against some of the most prominent figures pushing conspiracy theories, resulting in significant defamation rulings and damages against Alex Jones, who was bankrupted as a result.

In 2024, parody news site The Onion attempted to buy Infowars, hoping to undermine Jones' fake news by reframing it as satire. Victims' families supported the sale, but it was blocked by a judge – though The Onion will continue pushing for the deal to go through.

RADIO SHOW   NEWS   VIDEOS   STORE

WATCH LIVE

Infowars, an online news site run by Alex Jones (pictured above), spread
conspiracy theories that the Sandy Hook school shooting was faked.
Legal action was taken against Jones, ultimately leaving him bankrupt.

A deadly echo chamber

Social media platforms are often seen as channels of communication. But they can also be catalysts for conflict, as the Rohingya people in Myanmar know all too well. In 2017, Facebook unwittingly became the launching pad for a genocidal campaign against the Rohingya Muslim minority in the country. Fake news, hate speech and inflammatory posts spread rapidly, inciting violence and driving more than 700,000 Rohingya from their homes. According to Médicins sans Frontières, an estimated 10,000 Rohingya people were killed.

Facebook failed to curb the spread of harmful content, partly because it had few content moderators able to understand the language in which the hateful posts were written. Algorithms designed to promote engagement blindly amplified ethnic hatred, twisting a social network into an echo chamber of deadly propaganda.

In December 2021, the Rohingya filed a landmark lawsuit against Facebook, seeking £150 billion in damages. The case was eventually dismissed, but their plight is a chilling reminder: in the wrong hands, even social media designed to connect us can be used to divide, destroy and devastate communities.

A Rohingya refugee looks at Facebook on his phone after fleeing Myanmar in 2017. The Rohingya filed a landmark lawsuit against Facebook, accusing the platform of promoting hate speech.

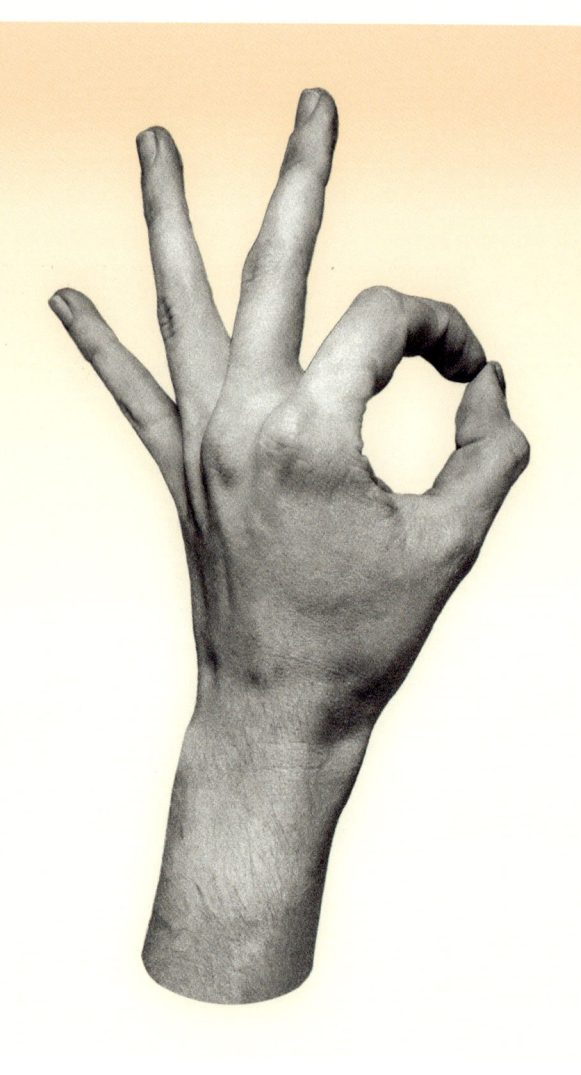

4chan users spread a rumour that the OK hand sign was a symbol of white power because of how the pinkie, ring and middle finger make a *W*, while the index and thumb form a *P*.

How 4chan seeds lies

Spend enough time on the internet, and you'll realise it's often not a nice place. But some parts of the web are less palatable than others. Case in point: the anonymous image board called 4chan. Set up in 2003, it hosts a range of forums where users can share images, but over the years, has acquired a reputation for abusive, far-right content – indeed, the term 'alt-right' (abbreviated from 'alternative right') to describe the largely online white nationalist movement was popularised on 4chan's infamous politics boards.

The anonymous nature of 4chan and its lack of moderation makes it a place where users like to cause mischief, as well as share racist, sexist and violent content among themselves. Its users enjoy hoodwinking the world and have done so multiple times.

4chan was where the Pizzagate conspiracy theory took off (more on this later), as well as disinformation about the use of the OK hand sign being a white supremacist symbol. 4chan's terminally online users might join the board to find like-minded people to banter with, but instead find themselves in a poisonous echo chamber where irony and hate speech are mixed up. The site attracts as many as 20 million unique users each month, but its cultural impact stretches beyond this, with things going viral away from its image board (the joking adoption of the OK symbol has since been co-opted by actual white supremacists).

The early deaths of Queen Elizabeth II

When Queen Elizabeth II's death was announced on television and via a missive by the Royal Family on 8 September 2022, it wasn't the first time the news had circulated. Rumours had spread on social media in 2016 that Queen Elizabeth had passed away after catching a severe cold. These claims, spurred by a series of misleading headlines and manipulated images, led to widespread misinformation until an official statement from Buckingham Palace clarified that the Queen was alive and well. That was just the first high-profile example involving the Queen. In 2020, a viral Twitter post, crafted to look like an official statement, falsely announced her death.

In both instances, the fake news created a ripple effect, highlighting the vulnerability of truth in the digital era. It showed how social media's speed and reach can turn misinformation into a seemingly credible narrative within minutes. But most worryingly, it also indicated how even the most carefully media-managed institutions can fall foul of social media's viral spread.

An assault on democracy

Donald Trump, the lying 'inventor' of fake news

It's a painful irony that one of the biggest liars in modern politics brought the term 'fake news' to the wider world. Donald Trump railed against the 'fake news media' throughout his 2016–2020 presidency, even claiming to have invented the phrase (he didn't; journalist Craig Silverman was using it as early as 2014). But after it left his lips in a January 2017 CNN interview, 'fake news' entered the pop culture lexicon, weaponised by Trump's supporters to dismiss unflattering coverage. Meanwhile, Trump spewed 30,573 misleading statements in his first presidential term – something critics called an authoritarian attack on truth itself.

Trump's awful brilliance lay in crunching the complex criticism of his actions into a punchy, memeable putdown tailor-made for the era of social media squabbles. With those two words, he shifted the terms of the debate and forced the world to reflect on the nature of facts and objectivity, ushering in the era of 'post-truth politics'. Yet his supporters ate up the terminology, revelling in the barbed jab at established authority. Call it fake, call it genius, but Trump's war cry will echo for years to come.

What happens when politics is 'post-truth'?

Barack Obama was a Muslim. Kamala Harris flip-flopped between her Indian and Black heritage when it suited her. These are two claims made by Donald Trump – and, for the avoidance of doubt, neither is true.

Yet, thanks to Trump and plenty of other politicians who put political expediency before human decency, our current political era is defined by a curious phrase: post-truth. It was Oxford Dictionaries' international word of the year in 2016, following a 20-fold increase in its use year-on-year. The word had been used for decades before, but the concept of setting aside the truth – or having different 'versions' of the truth, depending on your political persuasion – has never been so prevalent.

A post-truth political environment is one in which fake news abounds. People pick and choose their own 'facts', carefully chosen to advance their argument, while conveniently ignoring those that don't back up their claims. And if you don't have facts? Just make them up. Like Donald Trump.

Veles, Macedonia: the fake news capital of the world?

Veles, a small city of 40,000 inhabitants in Macedonia, may not seem like the locus of the fake news revolution. But people working in the city helped seed the world with fake news – and arguably helped sway the 2016 US presidential election. More than 140 websites, targeting political news junkies and peddling disinformation, sprung up from Veles thanks to enterprising entrepreneur Mirko Ceselkoski and others, many of whom were teenagers.

Ceselkoski and his colleagues created outlandish and factually incorrect content about the candidates in the 2016 US presidential election that enticed users to click on their websites, where they'd then be served adverts, the income from which would flow into the pockets of the Veles fake news writers. Some could make $5,000 a month – and had no qualms about poisoning the political well when there was money to be made. We can't know whether Ceselkoski's fake news put Trump in the White House the first time, but it certainly contributed to the distrust of political and media institutions that worked in his favour. Indeed, Ceselkoski printed business cards that read, 'THE MAN WHO HELPED DONALD TRUMP WIN US ELECTIONS'.

Russian interference in the 2016 US election

Macedonian fake news websites weren't the only ones meddling in the 2016 US election; more significantly, the Russian government, through its intelligence agencies, executed a multi-pronged strategy to sow confusion and influence the election's outcome. Russia hacked the Democratic National Committee's (DNC) emails, releasing sensitive information through WikiLeaks, aiming to undermine Hillary Clinton's campaign.

They did this through two state-linked hacking groups, nicknamed (strangely) Cozy Bear and Fancy Bear. Cozy Bear first found its way into the DNC's systems in 2015 and was tracking emails and releasing damaging snippets selectively chosen to disinform. Fancy Bear, which had previously hacked the German Bundestag, did the same thing since April 2016.

At the same time as those groups spread damaging falsehoods, troll farms (institutionalised groups paid to sow disinformation) run by Russia's Internet Research Agency fomented anger about the leaks through social media and news website comment sections. Whether it changed the course of the vote is uncertain. But, by casting a light on dabbling in foreign elections, it changed the course of history.

Pizza served at Comet Ping Pong Pizzeria in Washington, DC. The pizzeria became the centre of a conspiracy theory about a child trafficking scandal after it was mentioned in campaign trail emails leaked by Russian hackers.

A paedophile ring in a pizza shop

In 2016, WikiLeaks released emails from the Democratic National Committee, which oversees the election campaign of left-leaning politicians in the United States, like former Democratic presidential candidate Hillary Clinton. The leaks, linked to Russian hackers, had huge ramifications. But one unexpected aftershock was that it fuelled conspiracy theories about child abuse.

Nicknamed Pizzagate, the conspiracy alleged that a child sex-trafficking ring involving high-profile Democrats was operating out of the Comet Ping Pong pizzeria in Washington, DC. The theory took hold thanks to emails in campaign chairman John Podesta's inbox asking workers on the campaign trail whether they would like pizza or hot dogs (conspiracists claimed these were codewords for child trafficking).

It was, of course, false. However, online gossip had an offline impact: on 4 December 2016, Edgar Maddison Welch, a man who believed in the Pizzagate theory, entered the restaurant with a rifle, wanting to investigate the claims himself. Welch fired his gun inside the restaurant – luckily harming no one – and was arrested and imprisoned. And in a polarised election campaign that ultimately saw Hillary Clinton lose, who's to say what impact the conspiracy had on voting intention?

Jacob Chansley, a.k.a the QAnon Shaman, inside the US Capitol building. Chansley was part of the pro-Trump mob that rioted in the Capitol to protest President Biden's inaugeration in 2021.

The shadowy conspirator, QAnon

The notion of a Democrat-sponsored sex trafficking ring in a pizzeria in Washington, DC, didn't end with the 2016 election results. Instead, the conspiracy grew, evolving into a far-right political movement a year later: QAnon. Centring on claims made by a mysterious figure who signs his missives with the letter 'Q', the movement unifies several conspiracy theories, suggesting that an elite global cabal of paedophiles, cannibals and Satan-worshippers secretly controls governments around the world, and that Donald Trump is working to expose and defeat them.

The theory first appeared on 4chan (p.85) but has bled through to the mainstream, embraced by journalists like Liz Crokin and Fox News presenter Sean Hannity. The movement has even infiltrated religion, with QAnon theories being shared by Christian pastors and read at church services across America.

QAnon supporters were among those who attacked the US Capitol on 6 January 2021. Though it has roots in American politics, the movement is not confined to the US: there are QAnon Facebook pages in 71 countries worldwide.

Cracking down on fake news in China

Soon after Donald Trump first came to power in the United States, riding in on a wave of so-called 'fake news' accusations, China issued a law of its own to tackle the problem.

The country's Cybersecurity Law, passed in 2016, outlaws the creation or spreading of fake news that disturbs the economic and social order – placing the onus on both individuals and the social media platforms to prevent it from happening. Of course, in China, fake news means something different: it can encompass everything from baseless gossip to the sharing of information that embarrasses the ruling Communist Party.

Since then, others within China have called for the law to be further strengthened as the dissemination of disinformation evolves. But while China has been able to crack down on disinformation, other countries with greater freedom of speech and less of an iron grip on their citizens may struggle to define fake news in the first place.

A protestor in Beijing holds a blank piece of paper to symbolise their opposition to China's strict anti-Covid legislation, 2022. The blank piece of paper has become a symbol of Chinese oppression after strict censorship laws prevented protestors from writing slogans on their placards.

THE SCHOOL OF POPULISM

DONALD TRUMP
United States
of America

**RECEP TAYYIP
ERDOĞAN**
Türkiye

JAVIER MILEI
Argentina

GIORGIA MELONI
Italy

NARENDRA MODI
India

VIKTOR ORBÁN
Hungary

HERBERT KICKL
Austria

NIGEL FARAGE
United Kingdom

WILLIAM RUTO
Kenya

MARINE LE PEN
France

The unstoppable rise of populism

Populism – the political approach capitalising on a distinction between 'the people' and 'the elite' – is rising. An inherent distrust of this 'global elite' fuels the proliferation of fake news, rooted in the misguided belief that a powerful, secretive few manipulate global events for their benefit. This narrative taps into deep-seated fears, making it fertile ground for growing conspiracy theories.

The reason is simple: people feel powerless. When people feel disconnected from decision-making processes and sceptical of what they're being told, they seek alternative explanations. Often, these take the form of conspiracy theories, which offer simple, emotionally satisfying answers to complex issues. The internet amplifies these ideas, providing a platform for their rapid spread and reinforcing such beliefs. Fake news floods into that vacuum, preying on people's insecurities and worries. As a society, it's not just fake news we need to tackle; it's the widespread frustration with, and alienation from, our political systems, too.

Naomi Klein's 2023 book *Doppelganger* explored a phenomenon she dubbed the 'Mirror World': an unlikely digital alliance of far-right and 'far-out' (vaccine-sceptic hippies), thrown together by algorithms and united by their shared distrust of authority.

The Mirror World

Governments are poisoning your drinking water. Businesses are subliminally foisting diversity on us. Both are implausible, laughable ideas to most people – but in the Mirror World, a term coined by writer and activist Naomi Klein to describe an alternate reality crafted and perpetuated online, some believe these claims wholeheartedly.

That results in some very odd couples. The Mirror World can be fertile ground for what Klein describes as 'far-right meets the far out'. This unlikely convergence sees far-right, gun-toting Libertarians aligning with 'far out' wellness industry vaccine-sceptics, united by a shared distrust of institutional authority. Neither would have touched the other with a ten-foot bargepole in a pre-social media era. But lumped together by algorithmic chance that sees them fed the same anti-establishment posts, they become brothers in arms.

While these factions might have nothing in common on the surface, their shared distrust of government, media and science binds them in a powerful feedback loop, turning them into formidable agents of misinformation stretching across the political spectrum.

A pandemic of lies

The Covid-19 pandemic, which began in 2020, helped accelerate pre-existing societal trends, from the rise of online shopping to the preference for flexible working. But for many who consume fake news, it also deepened the rupture in reality and caused a proliferation of conspiracy theories – with dangerous consequences.

One of the most pernicious conspiracies claimed the virus was a bioweapon engineered in a lab. Despite extensive scientific evidence debunking this, the theory persisted, pushed by political rhetoric and viral social media posts. Donald Trump stood behind a White House podium and promoted drinking bleach to rid your body of the infection – a bad idea at any time – while others gave themselves diarrhoea by taking the anti-malaria drug hydroxychloroquine, falsely identified as a Covid cure.

Anti-vaccine misinformation also surged, with false claims about vaccine safety and efficacy discouraging many from getting vaccinated. The misinformation may have only originated from fringe groups, but it was amplified by social media algorithms designed to promote engaging content, regardless of its truth. 'Free speech warriors' refused the vaccine and disregarded social distancing, possibly contributing to a prolonging of the pandemic.

A man sporting a pro-Trump sweatband protests
the Covid lockdowns in California.

Political polarisation

Society has always been divided by politics. But never so much as it is now. In the US, where the system is dominated by two parties, a 2016 study found that a third of Democrat supporters believed Republicans were more unintelligent than the average person – and a third of Republicans had the same to say about Democrats. By 2022, half of each party's political supporters thought the other side were morons.

Fake news is both a cause and a consequence of this increasing political polarisation. When you feel like you have nothing in common with your opponents, you're more willing to sling mud at them – even if it's not based on fact – and more willing to believe fake news that paints them in an unsavoury light. Politics becomes pervaded by an 'us versus them' mentality, and critical thinking goes out the window, replaced by political point scoring.

And it's all amplified by social media, whose algorithms encourage us to shout our talking points past each other rather than talk to each other in a civilised manner. So don't be surprised if that survey number ticks ever higher in the coming years and the political divide widens to a chasm.

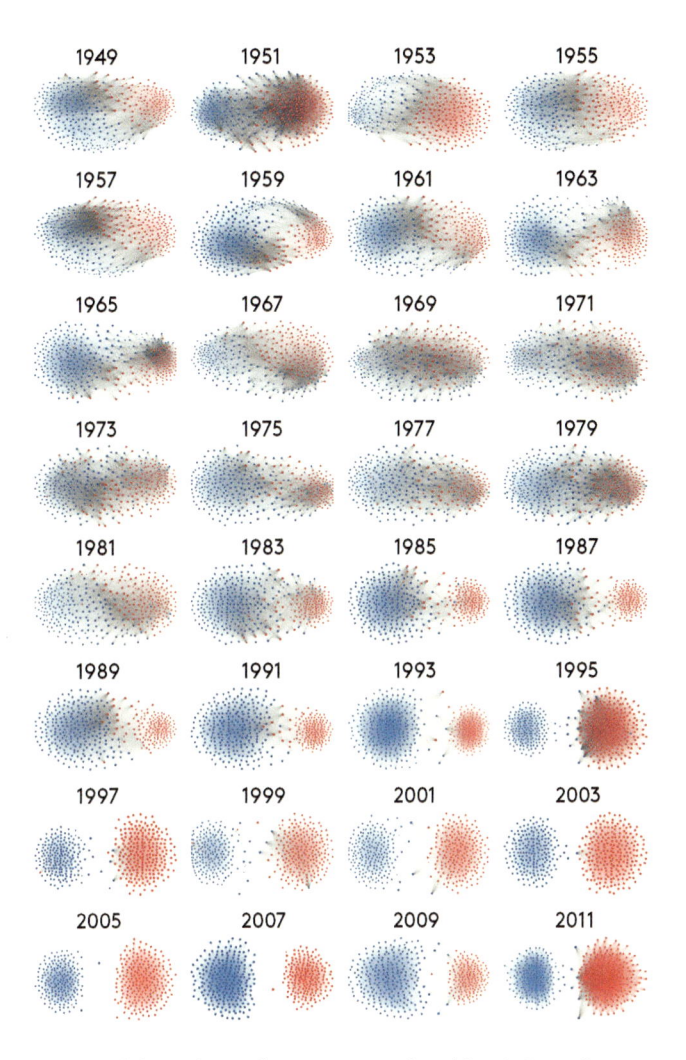

Each dot on this graph represents a member of the US House of Representatives from 1949 to 2012. Lines connecting the dots represent issues both members agree on. The maps show a gradual decline in cross-party agreement, with recent decades especially polarised.

The future of
fake news

How AI changes everything

Before the arrival of generative AI (the creation of new content based on text prompts, popularised by the release of ChatGPT in November 2022), creating fake news took time, effort and money.

Take the Internet Research Agency, the Russian army unit put to work to try and sway public opinion around the 2016 US presidential election (p.96). Real staff were employed to work in a physical office, typing out fake news designed to divide the populace.

With the advent of generative AI, that physical labour is no longer needed. Now, fake news peddlers can employ several tools to produce fictitious content on a previously unimaginable scale. Nor is this power limited to text alone: a new wave of tech-powered AI image and video generators makes it possible to produce convincing deepfakes in an instant. Multiple contradictory and competing narratives can be seeded, causing confusion and making it impossible to know what is real… and what is fake.

The Pope in a puffer jacket

It's not implausible for a man of a certain age living in Italy to don a sweeping, all-white Balenciaga puffer jacket for a jaunt on the streets of Rome. But it is a rather unexpected look for Pope Francis, pictured doing just this in a photograph from March 2023.

The 'Balenciaga Pope', or 'Pope in a puffer jacket' as it came to be known, was an image created using the artificial intelligence image generation tool Midjourney. Chicago labourer Pablo Xavier had been experimenting with the tool while high on magic mushrooms. He posted it online, labelled as being made with AI, but the context was quickly stripped away.

The media firestorm that erupted after the image went viral chastened Xavier. He now believes there should be regulations to limit the technology's use. 'I was just blown away,' he said of the image's reaction, 'I didn't want it to blow up like that.'

An AI-generated image of Pope Francis, the leader of the Catholic Church, wearing a Balenciaga puffer jacket. The image was created by Pablo Xavier using the image generation tool Midjourney.

Vladimir Putin, Taylor Swift and deepfaked videos

Seeing is believing – or so you'd think. But the advent of deepfake AI technology means it's no longer possible to trust what you see or hear. Using AI to create deepfakes of prominent politicians can put words in their mouths – as evidenced by one example, where footage of Vladimir Putin declaring martial law after Ukrainian troops crossed into Russia, was broadcast on television channels in June 2023.

The footage was fake. Ukraine hadn't lodged a counter-invasion. And Putin hadn't said that martial law would be in place. But it was convincing – and highlighted the danger and peril of deepfakes.

But deepfakes aren't limited to causing conflict on the battlefield alone: they're used to try and bring down celebrities through disrepute. Taylor Swift found herself the victim of deepfaked pornographic imagery, as misogynistic fans sought to produce salacious images of her with her boyfriend Travis Kelce using popular apps – showing how the tech can have an all too real human impact.

A deepfake is a realistic image, video or audio created using AI. Deepfaked pornographic videos of Taylor Swift and her boyfriend were viewed millions of times online, prompting calls for laws to criminalise the creation of deepfaked imagery.

Head of Facebook, Mark Zuckerberg, told Congress in 2018 that he was 'responsible for' not preventing the social media platform from being used for harm, including fake news, foreign interference in elections and hate speech (as was the case in Myanmar).

Can social media platforms be gatekeepers of fact?

Social media platforms have historically shied away from being arbiters of truth, partly because truth itself is a complicated concept. But there's another reason: it's not in their interests. Businesses have made billions from designing successful social media platforms and don't want to risk alienating their audience.

The executives at these companies often claim the platforms are little more than digital mirrors reflecting lies told by their users. But it's undeniable that social media has an outsized impact on our discourse. Before buying Twitter in 2022, Elon Musk called it the 'de facto public town square', which – considering town squares' historic role as the site of rallies and executions – says all you need to know about how influential he thought the platform was. Since then, X (as it is now called) has become a wellspring of conspiracies and lies.

In January 2025, Mark Zuckerberg announced that Meta (the company behind Facebook and Instagram) would stop fact-checking content. Instead, it would adopt a model similar to that used by X, where accuracy judgements are left up to users. The decision was criticised as a cynical move designed to appeal to Trump as he begins his second term. It's dangerous, too; as we've seen in Myanmar, failure to step in and adjudicate on disinformation can be a matter of life and death (p.82).

How to detect fake news

In this challenging, 'post-truth' world (p.92), with our democratic processes under threat and fake news fanning the flames of discontent, equipping people with the ability to detect and downplay fake news is more important than ever. But putting aside your own beliefs and getting to the heart of the matter can be tricky.

Some playbooks that help identify dis- or misinformation, and most highlight the importance of media literacy. Checking and considering the provenance of any information is a good first step: once you know where it comes from, you can better assess why someone might have chosen to publish or share it. Keeping a sceptical eye on what you see is also important. Fake news is designed to poke at your emotions; keep them in check to avoid falling foul. Cross-checking content with existing information, and particularly verifying the facts, is a strong defence against disinformation, too.

How to bring fake news to heel

Defining fake news in a regulatory way is a challenge. How do you know when something has been shared or spread deliberately? As a result, historically, laws tackling disinformation have been few and far between, with the government focusing on issues *caused* by fake news rather than the disinformation itself.

But legislation to outlaw the spreading of false or misleading information is growing, although it's not always a good thing. Between 2011 and 2022, 78 countries passed laws designed to limit fake news, with many of them enacted in the last few years, according to the Centre for International Media Assistance. The problem is that while some are laser-focused on what many would consider true 'fake news' (such as deliberately slandering an individual with knowingly false information), others are designed to give governments the ability to tamp down on criticism and stifle press freedom – a similar model to China (p.102).

There are glimmers of hope. Media literacy – teaching kids to spot fake news – is being introduced as a mandatory part of the curriculum in schools in California, Finland and elsewhere. Arguably, as technology creating and disseminating fake news becomes more sophisticated, so does our ability to detect it.

There is no Internet connection

Try:
- Putting your phone away.
- Going outside and touching grass.
- Speaking to a human face to face.

FAKENEWS_PROBE_FINISHED_NO_INTERNET

The future of fake news?

The ability to identify truth from falsehoods will get even harder, thanks to growing technologies that facilitate the production and dissemination of fake news. Generative AI tools like ChatGPT and Midjourney have shown that we can't trust what we see. We're being peppered with more information from an overflow of content daily and asked to make snap judgements on whether we believe them or not.

All this is happening while the concept of truth is increasingly up for debate. The word is mutating in meaning, and people are choosing to weaken its definition, bit by bit, by discussing different kinds and versions of 'truth'.

But it's worth noting that although technological developments have made it more pernicious, disinformation is not a new problem. From deliberate falsehoods to accidental rumours or jokes that get out of hand, this jaunt through the history of fake news shows that the information environment has always been a minefield. In the words of journalism professor Tom Rosenstiel: 'Misinformation is not like a plumbing problem you fix. It is a social condition, like crime, that you must constantly monitor and adjust to.' As the information we have access to has increased over time, humans have learnt to become more discerning consumers. Our natural appetite for dubious stories may never cease, but we can adjust our ways of dealing with them.